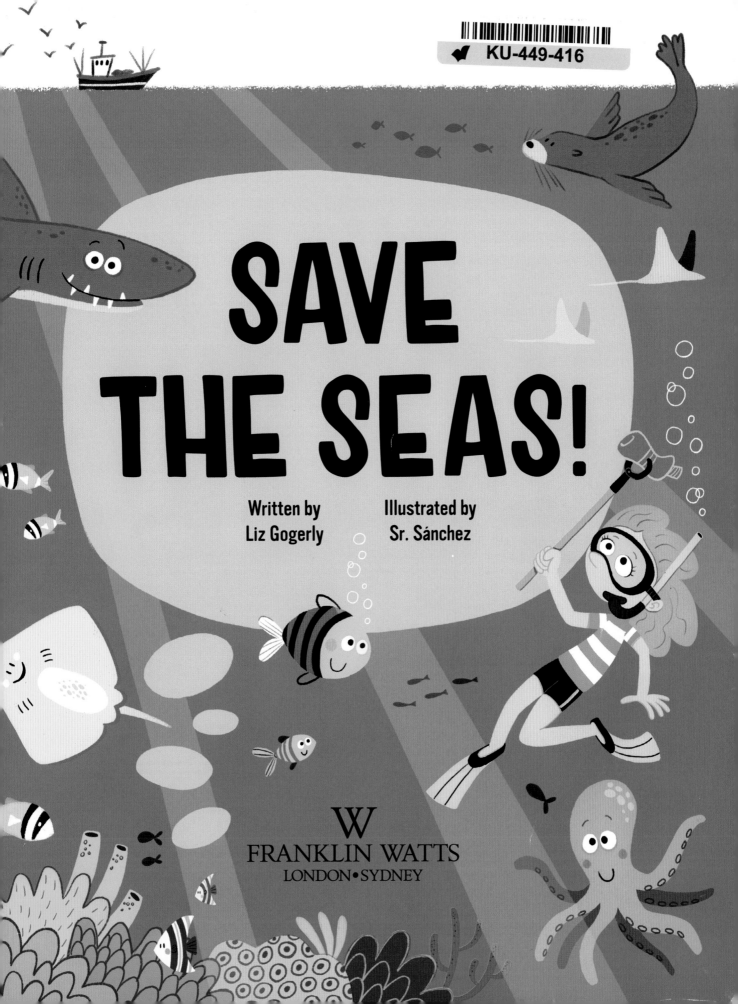

SAVE THE SEAS!

Written by
Liz Gogerly

Illustrated by
Sr. Sánchez

W
FRANKLIN WATTS
LONDON·SYDNEY

Franklin Watts

First published in Great Britain in 2021
by The Watts Publishing Group
© The Watts Publishing Group 2021

Managing editor: Victoria Brooker
Design: Anthony Hannant (Little Red Ant)

ISBN: 978 1 4451 7391 7 (hbk)
ISBN: 978 1 4451 7392 4 (pbk)

Printed in Dubai

Franklin Watts
An imprint of Hachette Children's Group
Part of The Watts Publishing Group
Carmelite House
50 Victoria Embankment
London EC4Y 0DZ
An Hachette UK Company

www.hachette.co.uk
www.franklinwatts.co.uk

MIX
Paper from
responsible sources
FSC
www.fsc.org
FSC® C104740

Contents

The Shell Hunters

The children are staying with Anjali's Aunt May who lives beside the sea. Down on the beach the tide is out and they are hunting for shells. As they sift through the piles of flotsam and jetsam they look for driftwood too. In the rock pools there is seaweed and pebbles.

Unfortunately, the children find plenty of plastic.

Mason finds a worn-out flip flop.

Oh yuk!

How did this end up here?

Anjali discovers a toothbrush in a rock pool.

Noah thinks he's collected a pile of beautiful shell pieces. He looks closer and finds half of it is plastic fragments.

Not so pretty after all!

Lulu finds an old plastic straw.

This shouldn't be here.

SEA FACT

A sea turtle with a plastic straw stuck in its nose went viral on the Internet in 2015. The suffering of this animal raised awareness about the dangers of plastic straws – they are now banned in many countries around the world. Since then, photographs of the plight of sea creatures, including seabirds feeding their chicks toothpicks or fish swimming in a cloud of plastic, have revealed what's going on in our oceans Scientists estimate that all baby turtles have plastic in their stomachs.

5

The Ghostly Nets

It's a dark night and the children are sitting around the fire with Aunt May. They can hear the waves crashing on to the shore. It's the perfect time to tell ghost stories …

Aunt May has the scariest story of all and it's about 'ghost nets'. These are abandoned fishing nets that are left at sea. They are almost invisible to sea creatures which can get trapped and die or become injured. Many nets get snagged on rocks or on coral reefs. Others get tangled with other plastic. Wherever they end up they are dangerous to marine life.

SEA FACT

Discarded crab traps, lobster pots, drift nets, deep-sea trawl nets and other fishing gear are other examples of deadly debris that ends up in our oceans. A crab trap captures more than just crabs! Marine specialists estimate that 10 per cent of the plastic waste in our oceans is discarded nets.

Most fishing nets are made from nylon or plastic which take years to decompose.

This means they remain underwater posing a threat to all kinds of creatures for a long time. Sharks, whales, dolphins, turtles, crustaceans and seabirds all get caught in the ghost nets!

Anjali wonders how we can limit the damage from nets. Aunt May explains that some fishermen now only use nets made from biodegradable materials. Others are changing the way they fish and not using nets. However, there needs to be more rules and regulations to ensure that nets do not end up in the sea at all.

The Tide is High

The next morning the children return to the beach. The sea is lapping up against the rocks and all the sand has disappeared under the waves. Everyone is disappointed. Aunt May explains that in around twelve hours the tide will go out and they will be able to beachcomb.

The Tide Cycle

The rise and fall of the tide is called the tide cycle. This shifting of the sea is mostly down to the Moon which has its own gravity that pulls (gravitational pull) the oceans towards it to cause high tides.

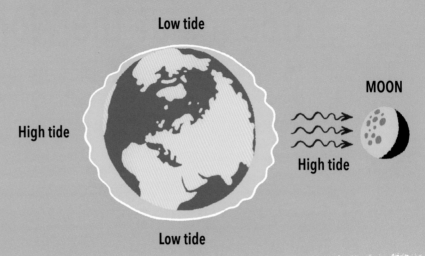

The Moon's gravitational pull causes high tides on the side of Earth closest to the Moon, and furthest away.

Low tide

High tide

MOON

High tide

Low tide

The Tide is Low

After lunch the sea has gone out again and the children run around on the golden sand. Later, they gather plastic rather than shells. Lulu is sifting through a pile of seaweed when she spots a baby seal. Aunt May tells everyone to stand well back as they can bite. The pup looks like it's lost its mother so they call a local wildlife organisation to come and help. Sometimes the sea washes up more than we expect!

Oceans of the World

The children are at school. They meet their new teacher, Ms Barker, who tells them they will be learning more about the sea this term.

Sea or Ocean?

A sea is a smaller part of an ocean and is usually found in areas where the ocean and land meet.

Estuaries

Mangrove forests

Salt marshes

Rocky shores

ATLANTIC OCEAN

PACIFIC OCEAN

Ms Barker explains that the ocean is an ecosystem that covers over 70 per cent of the Earth. It's so enormous we could never explore all of it. But, that mighty body of water provides us with drinking water, food, energy and even medicine. Our seas are amazing and we need to look after them!

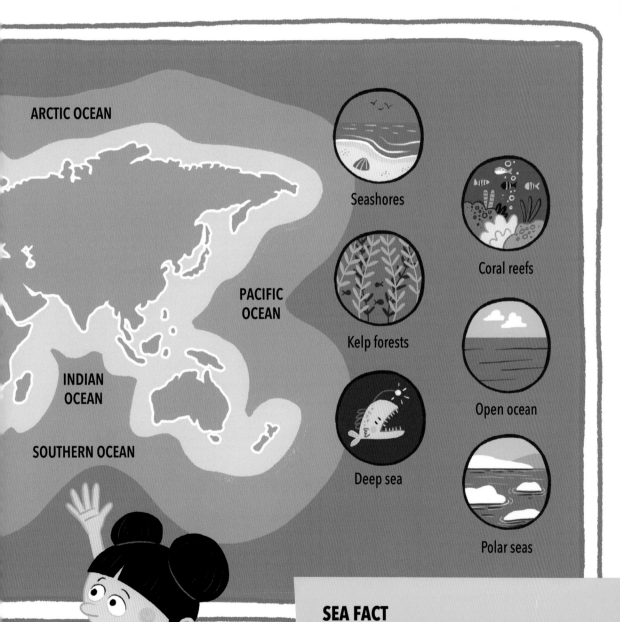

ARCTIC OCEAN

PACIFIC OCEAN

INDIAN OCEAN

SOUTHERN OCEAN

Seashores

Coral reefs

Kelp forests

Open ocean

Deep sea

Polar seas

SEA FACT

The ocean is deeper than the highest mountains on Earth. The Mariana Trench is the deepest point in the North Pacific Ocean and the deepest point in any ocean. If Mount Everest were submerged here, it would be covered by over 2 km of water!

Sunlit, Twilight and Midnight Zones

Ms Barker loves the ocean! She's a surfer so her favourite bit is the waves – especially if they're big and powerful and she can ride the wave to the shore. Sometimes she gets wiped out, which means she goes under the water. It's another world down there with different zones ...

EUPHOTIC ZONE ◄

The top layer is the **euphotic zone**. Sunlight reaches this zone, which means that seaweed, algae, phytoplankton, mangroves and seagrass can grow here. Plenty of food means abundant marine life, such as sharks, whales, dolphins, turtles and jellyfish.

DISPHOTIC ZONE ►

The **disphotic zone** receives hardly any sunlight so it's also called the twilight ocean. There is hardly any light which means plants won't grow. All living things have to eat what falls from above or prey on other creatures. Squid, octopus, swordfish, cuttlefish and eels are found here. Some of the fish here are bioluminescent, which means they create their own light to hunt for food.

APHOTIC ZONE ►

The **aphotic zone** is also known as the midnight ocean, because it is the deepest and darkest part of the ocean. There isn't much to eat down here and many of the creatures are predators, lying in wait ready to snap almost anything that gets in their way! Many use bioluminescent light to lure their prey. Gulper eels, slickheads, bristlemouths and phantom anglerfish are just some of the creatures at this depth.

200 m

200 m – 1,000 m

1,000 m – 4,000 m

CREATE LAYERS OF THE SEA

What you need:

Equipment

A clean glass

A jar with a lid

A bowl and spoon
for mixing

Black treacle

Blue food colouring,
cooking oil and water

Sticky labels and pen

Instructions:

1) Pour the treacle into the jar until it's
   about 1/3 full.

2) In the bowl, add drops of blue food
   colouring to some water until you've
   made a dark blue colour.

3) Pour this mixture carefully into the jar
   until the jar is about 2/3 full. The mixture
   should sit on top of the treacle.

4) In the bowl, add a few drops of blue
   food colouring to the cooking oil to
   make a light blue mixture.

5) Carefully pour
   this mixture into
   the jar so it sits on
   top of the water
   mixture below.

6) You have just
   created the layers
   of the sea. Now
   you can label each
   layer as shown in
   the picture.

SUNLIGHT

TWILIGHT

MIDNIGHT

What's for Dinner in the Sea?

Ms Barker has organised a school trip to an aquarium. Noah can't wait to see the octopus – it can taste what it touches with its arms! Lulu is looking forward to watching the seahorses – they have to eat around 30-50 times a day.

This aquarium is filled with marine life from all over the world. The staff know how to care for each and every creature properly. They create the best living environment and provide food with the right nutrients. The children watch some animals being fed …

This giant Pacific octopus is most active at night so the keeper gently wakes her up to feed her. Instantly, she changes colour and goes from grey to red! She likes to gobble up crabs, clams, shrimp and fish. ▼

These seahorses are fed frozen shrimp.

In the ocean they would eat plankton too. They make a loud clicking noise as they eat … ▶

14

These lemon sharks are fed a mixture of mussels, prawns, mackerel and other fish. The keeper explains that these sharks are so well fed that they don't go for the live fish swimming around them. ▼

The cheeky Gentoo penguins waddle over for some tasty fish. The keeper feeds them by hand so he can keep an eye on their health and make sure they are well. ▼

Whale Tales and Marine Meals

The seas are filled with some fascinating creatures. Sadly, our amazing marine life is in danger because of what they're eating ...

Lulu reads a sad story about a whale washed up on the beach. It had eaten over 100 kg of litter, including plastic bags, nylon rope and even plastic cups! The plastic had formed into a hard ball that had blocked the whale's stomach so it couldn't eat.

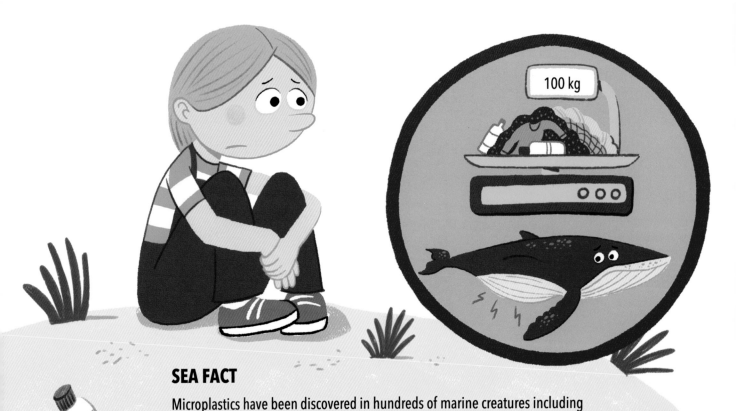

100 kg

SEA FACT

Microplastics have been discovered in hundreds of marine creatures including fish, dolphins and seals. The fish that humans eat is sometimes contaminated with microplastics too. Microplastics come from:

- larger plastic that has broken down over time
- microbeads, that are found in some health and beauty products, such as toothpaste and face creams
- microfibres from fabric and clothing, which are shed when things are washed.

Noah discovers that the plastic he collected on the beach isn't the only danger to animals. Microplastics are less than 5 mm in size and marine creatures are mistaking them for food and gobbling them up …

OCEAN FOOD CHAINS

The ocean food chain begins with phytoplankton. Phytoplankton use photosynthesis to convert energy from the Sun into food energy. Phytoplankton pass along the food chain to zooplankton. Zooplankton include tiny organisms, such as krill and shrimp-like creatures.

PHYTOPLANKTON + ZOOPLANKTON = PLANKTON

Plankton is the key to all life in the oceans. It is eaten by all kinds of creatures from tiny fish, sea snails and crabs to large creatures, such as jellyfish and enormous whale sharks.

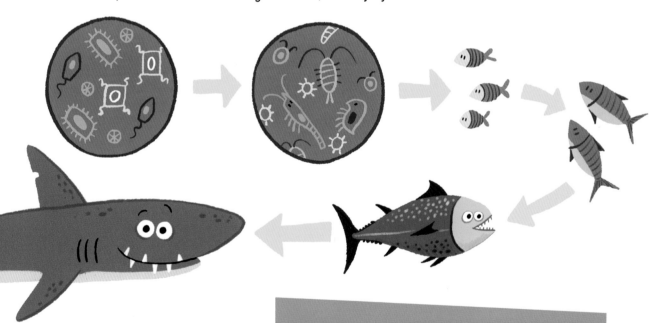

Look at the diagram above to see how food energy can be passed along the ocean food chain. Small fish are often dinner for the big fish!

OCEAN ACTION

The only way we can stop the threat of microplastics is to reduce the plastic that is released into our seas. Even if you live far away from seas and oceans, you can help by reducing, reusing and recycling as much plastic as possible. When you're out and about, take your litter home with you.

Climate Change and our Oceans

When the children go to the beach on a windy day, the waves are enormous and crash over the seawall. On days like these, Anjali can see there's a connection between the weather and the sea.

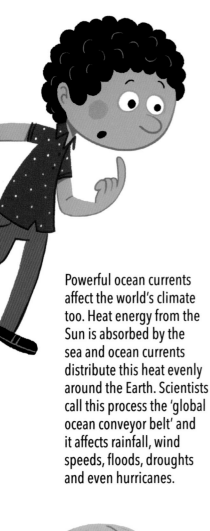

Powerful ocean currents affect the world's climate too. Heat energy from the Sun is absorbed by the sea and ocean currents distribute this heat evenly around the Earth. Scientists call this process the 'global ocean conveyor belt' and it affects rainfall, wind speeds, floods, droughts and even hurricanes.

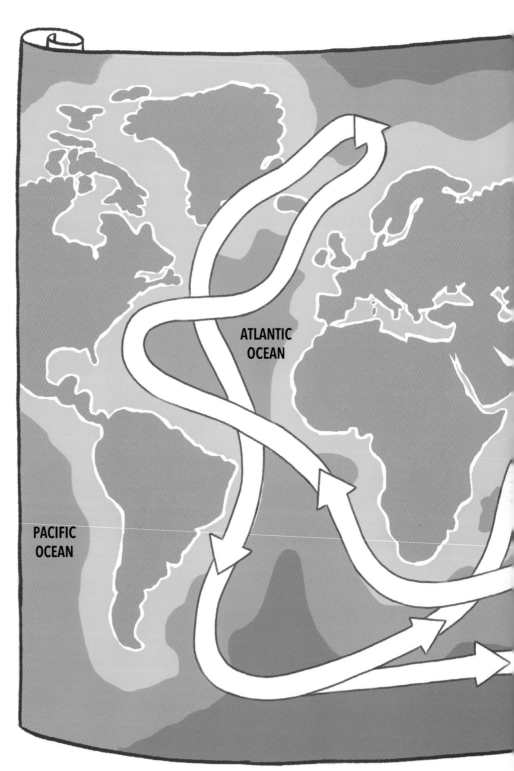

ATLANTIC
OCEAN

PACIFIC
OCEAN

Scientists have discovered that because of global warming our oceans are gradually rising in temperature. Warmer seas are slowly changing ocean currents which means weather patterns are disrupted. In the future, scientists predict stronger storms and hurricanes with greater rainfall.

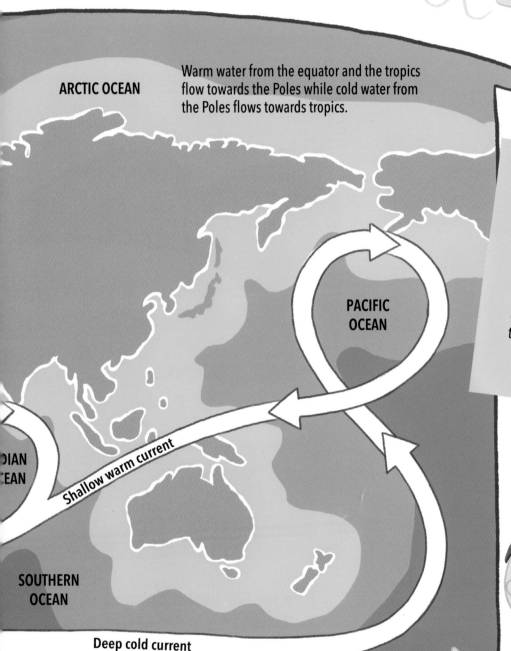

ARCTIC OCEAN

Warm water from the equator and the tropics flow towards the Poles while cold water from the Poles flows towards tropics.

PACIFIC OCEAN

INDIAN OCEAN

Shallow warm current

SOUTHERN OCEAN

Deep cold current

SEA FACT

The global ocean conveyor belt broke down around 950,000 years ago, possibly causing a series of ice ages. Some scientists think that our ocean currents are slowing down because of climate change. Nobody knows whether this will cause another ice age.

What happens when the Sea Rises?

Anjali is keen to do her bit to fight climate change. She has volunteered with a local environmental group. Lily has been a member of the group for years and she explains the problems caused by rising sea levels to Anjali.

Facts and Figures

All around the world sea levels are rising. Global warming has caused global sea levels to rise by around 23 cm since 1880. Sea levels have risen quicker in the last 25 years. Every year the sea rises by around 3.2 mm.

How are Sea Levels Rising?

Glaciers and ice sheets are thawing as the Earth warms up. Icebergs and floating ice at sea are also melting. Water is released from these and flows into the sea. Water expands as the oceans warm up.

Animals in Danger

Polar bears live on sea ice in the Arctic Ocean. As the ice melts the polar bears struggle to get to places where they can find food to survive. Turtles, seals and other animals nest, give birth and raise their young on sandy beaches. Rising sea levels will mean many creatures will lose their natural habitats. Animals will have to compete for smaller spaces and so their numbers will decline.

Humans in Danger

Humans are suffering too. Floods have devastated the city of Venice, Italy. Homes are damaged and tourism is badly affected. Venice has been under water countless times, but when the city was flooded in 2019, a record-breaking 85 per cent of the city was affected. Oceans are going to keep rising, which means many more animals and places will be at risk in the future. Countries like Bangladesh, parts of the USA such as Florida, and cities such as Venice, may one day be covered by sea.

Coral Reefs in Danger

Noah's big brother Josh has been diving at the Great Barrier Reef in Australia. He tells Noah all about it in one of his messages (see below).

Noah wants to know what is causing this bleaching. He discovers that when the sea warms up by just 1°C then bleaching can occur. The colourful algae that live within the coral leave when it gets too hot so the coral turns white. If the temperatures remain high then the algae do not come back and the coral dies.

Hey Noah,

Wow, the coral reef is awesome – so colourful and full of life. I've seen manta rays, sea turtles and even a dugong! Sadly, other parts of the reef are 'bleached' and look completely white. It's really eerie because there are no fish. We have to save these beautiful reefs!

Love, Josh xx

The Great Barrier Reef

In Australia, the Great Barrier Reef suffered terrible damage to its coral reef in 1980, 1982, 1992, 1994, 1998, 2002, 2006, 2016 and 2017. Scientists now fear that these bleaching events will happen every year so there is no opportunity for the coral to grow back.

AUSTRALIA

Great Barrier Reef

Acid Ocean

Noah also finds out that acidification is damaging coral and other marine life. Greenhouse gases, such as carbon dioxide, released into the atmosphere are absorbed by the sea. This changes the chemistry of our oceans making the water more acidic. Zooplankton and the whole ocean food chain upwards are suffering from the effects of acidification.

Exploring our Seas

Lulu is reading about sea explorers of the past. Throughout history, the mighty and powerful seas and oceans have fascinated humans.

In ancient times the Phoenicians, the Greeks, the Romans, the Vikings and the Chinese took to the seas on a quest to find new lands.

Christopher ▶
Columbus

The Norse explorer Leif Eriksen is believed to have crossed the Atlantic Ocean to become the first European in North America in around 1002.

At the beginning of the 15th century Chinese fleets explored the China Sea and Indian Ocean.

Later in the 15th century the explorer Christopher Columbus sailed across the Atlantic Ocean to explore Asia. In fact, he landed in the Americas and claimed he'd discovered the 'New World' – even though it was already inhabited.

Leif
Eriksen ▶

Ferdinand ▶
Magellan

Many people have attempted to circumnavigate (go around) the world by boat. Portuguese explorer Ferdinand Magellan is probably the first known person to sail around the world on his expedition of 1519–1522. The French explorer Jeanne Baret became the first woman to circumnavigate the world in 1766, although she had to disguise herself as a man to do so.

Francois Gabart ▼

◄ Jeanne Baret

Krystyna ▲
Chojnowska-Liskiewicz

In 1976 Krystyna Chojnowska-Liskiewicz became the first woman to sail around the world single-handed. New Zealand's Naomi James was attempting to break the record at the same time, but Krystyna just beat her.

Naomi James ▼

Laura Dekker ▲

Sixteen-year-old Laura Dekker became the youngest sailor to circumnavigate the world. She set off in 2010 and it took her 17 months. French sailor Francois Gabart took just 42 days to sail around the world in 2017, breaking the record for the fastest solo expedition.

SEA FACT

In the past, people wanted to explore the world or break new records. Now many sailors want to save the seas! Laura Dekker supports a society which actively protects oceans and marine life. The society's fleet of boats tackle illegal activities that pose a danger to our seas or sea creatures. Francois Gabart uses his knowledge and love of the sea to campaign against climate change.

Surfers who Save the Seas

Ms Barker is on a beach clean with the rest of her surfing friends. As they scoop up rubbish they get talking about the biggest waves in the world and which surfers have attempted to ride these monster waves …

OCEAN ACTION

These days surfers are encouraged to buy surfboards made with more renewable materials rather than plastics. Surfers should look out for boards made with recycled material where possible too!

The surfer who has conquered the most monster waves is Kelly Slater of the USA. This surfing superhero came first in the World Surfing Championships 11 times and is often called the greatest surfer of all time. He's also a keen supporter of an environmental group which organises beach cleans and educates people about protecting our beaches and seas.

HOW DOES A SURFBOARD FLOAT?

A surfboard is less dense than the water underneath it, therefore it can float. Seas and oceans are very salty. This simple activity shows you how salt affects the density of water.

What you need:

2 tall glasses big enough to hold an egg

Warm water

Salt

Two eggs

A ruler

A tablespoon

Instructions:

1) Fill the two glasses with warm water about 3/4 full.

2) Mix 3 tablespoons of salt into one glass and stir to dissolve the salt.

3) Gently lower an egg into each glass.

4) Use a ruler to measure how high each egg floats.

The egg in the glass with the salt water should float. Adding salt to water makes the water denser and adds mass (more weight) to the water. This makes the water denser and so more objects will float.

Monster Waves

Noah has another message from his brother Josh who's just experienced some of the biggest waves in his life!

Monster Waves

Noah has discovered that mega waves seem to come out of nowhere even when the sea is calm. Rogue waves, freak waves or monster waves are a danger talked about by fishermen for centuries. Scientists have only recently started to research these deadly waves that can reach over 30 m high.

Hey Noah,
I'm on the beautiful island of Bali now. It's like paradise here except today I got soaked by some unexpected, enormous waves! The lifeguard says it's because of a storm in the Pacific. The storms are getting wilder and so are the waves!

Love, Josh xx

The Draupner Wave or 'New Year Wave' was the first recorded monster wave. This mighty wave struck on 1 January 1995 on the Draupner gas platform in the North Sea off Norway. The wave measured 25.6 m, which is about the same as a seven-storey building. ▶

Large waves

Is the world getting wetter and wilder? Scientists believe global warming is making storms at sea more powerful. Hurricanes and typhoons are stronger and more destructive than ever. Storm surges are getting worse because of rising sea levels too.

Storm surge

Tsunamis

At school, Noah tells Ms Barker and the others about the rogue waves. Ms Barker tells them that today they're going to be finding out about some other monstrous sea waves called tsunamis.

Tsunamis are great walls of water which, when they hit land, can wipe out entire communities and can kill thousands of people. These powerful waves are caused by earthquakes, landslides or volcanoes erupting under the sea. The shift on the ocean floor causes the water to rise and form a tsunami.

Tsunamis are HUGE waves.

Some scientists suggest there is a connection between climate change and tsunamis. Tsunamis occur because of earthquakes at sea but some scientists believe that earthquakes may be triggered by climate change. Global warming is contributing to rising sea levels which in turn could lead to more devastating tsunamis in the future.

SEA FACT

The highest tsunami ever recorded was at Lituya Bay, Alaska, in 1958. It measured over 30 m high. The Indian Ocean tsunami of 2004 is the deadliest yet, killing over 230,000 people. It was caused by an earthquake measuring 9.1 (10 is the highest) on the Richter scale under the ocean.

UPWARD WAVE

EARTHQUAKE EPICENTRE

FAULT LINE

OCEAN ACTION

It's difficult to understand how the little things we do can make a difference to those mighty waves, but if everyone makes changes in their life then together we can tackle climate change and global warming. Jump on your bike or walk rather than asking for a lift. Put on a jumper instead of turning up the heating. And always switch off the lights.

Sea Power

Just the thought of tsunamis and monster waves gives the children goosebumps, imagining the power of those enormous waves. Ms Barker tells the children that engineers have already found ways to generate energy from the waves of the sea - it is called ocean wave energy. However, the technology is expensive and isn't widely used yet.

The power of the waves can be captured in three ways.

1. Devices on the surface of the sea capture power as the waves move up and down.

Hinged floats

Water surface

At the moment most of the world's energy is generated from fossil fuels, such as oil, natural gas and coal. Burning these non-renewable sources releases carbon into the atmosphere (carbon emissions), which is contributing to global warming. The sea is a massive renewable source of energy. It's exciting to think that one day the sea will meet some of the world's energy needs.

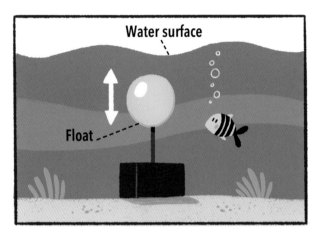

2. The movement of the waves causes underwater pistons to move up and down. This movement is harnessed to make electricity.

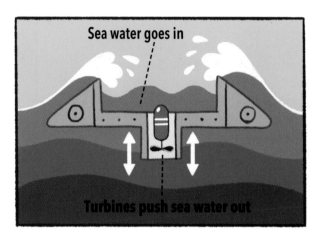

3. Water is captured in reservoirs built on the coastline. The water is pumped back to sea through turbines to produce energy.

SEA FACT

Tidal energy is another form of energy we can generate from the sea. The movement of the sea as the tide goes in and out makes underwater turbines spin to generate electricity.

The Sea's Greatest Mysteries

The children have been watching a documentary about the ocean and it's got them thinking. It's amazing how little we really know and understand about our seas.

Mason is in awe of the milky seas that glow so much that you can see them on satellite photos from space. The milky glow, also called luminescence, has been seen all over the world. The light created by the bacteria is blue, not the milky white it appears, which just adds to the mystery!

Denmark Strait

Iceland

Greenland

Warm water flow

Cold water sinks

Cold water overflows

Anjali wants to discover more about the terrain of the mysterious seafloor. There are underwater volcanoes lurking below as well as waterfalls. The world's largest underwater waterfall is found in the Denmark Strait. Cold water falls over a huge drop to the ocean floor. Nobody really understands how it can happen.

OCEAN ACTION

There are many more amazing creatures in our oceans and on our shorelines for you to discover. Giant squid 'Kraken' or the giant oarfish are just some of the mysterious creatures – look them up in books and on the Internet. What strange creatures will you find?

Noah is fascinated with sea creatures. The immortal jellyfish is one of his favourites. It is found in warm waters all over the world. It gets its name because it never dies. Once the jellyfish reaches maturity it shrinks and sinks to the bottom of the ocean where it begins its life cycle again.

Lulu is interested in dugongs and manatees. These gentle giants are also called 'sea cows' but they aren't the same species. In the past sailors mistook these slow-moving animals for mermaids. It's true they do have eyes like human beings but just look at those noses!

SEA FACT

Nobody knows how many creatures there are living in our seas. Around 242,500 marine species have been identified, but there are believed to be between 500,000 and 10 million marine species. Every year about 2,000 species are discovered and recorded.

Fighting Pollution to Save the Seas

Our oceans seem mighty and extraordinary so what can we do as individuals to save them?

We can help protect the precious biodiversity of our oceans by tackling plastic pollution.

Mason always takes his reusable shopping bag out with him when he goes shopping for his parents.

I don't want a plastic bag I've used to trap or kill any creature.

Even small changes can save the lives of marine animals.

SEA FACT
Around 8.3 billion plastic straws wash up on the beaches each year. Giving up plastic straws is one of the easiest things you can do and a big help to the environment.

Lulu doesn't use plastic straws ever! There are alternatives made from paper, metal or glass but she'd rather do without ...

Oil pollution is also harming the biodiversity of our oceans. Oil spills from tankers or leaks from oil pipes poison and kill all kinds of marine life. Wildlife habitats, such as beaches or mangrove forests, can become uninhabitable for years. Oil from our cars ends up in the ocean too. The oil that drips onto our roads eventually seeps back to the sea – it is called run-off pollution.

We've beaten the microbead in our home!

It's a 'step' in the right direction.

Anjali is on a mission to ban microplastics in her home. She tells her mum to read the ingredients of any cleaning products, cosmetics and toiletries very carefully before she buys anything.

Noah walks or cycles rather than jumping in the car or bus. It's a small way of reducing oil consumption. If everybody did the same then there'd be a lot less oil on the roads.

REDUCE > REUSE >

You may live near or far from the sea but there are things we can all do to help the survival of this precious ecosystem. The children have made changes in their own lives.

Noah has encouraged all his friends and family to cycle when they can. His family share their car with friends too. REDUCING their carbon emissions from cars will help slow down climate change which will help save the seas ...

Mason is on a mission to REUSE things rather than throw them away. His football boots don't fit him any more so he's given them to another boy in his football team ...

RECYCLE > RETHINK

It takes energy in factories to make everything we use or wear. Then there is the energy needed for transportation of those goods too. By reusing and recycling we are saving energy in both ways.

Anjali is wearing sunglasses made from RECYCLED ocean plastic. It feels good to be green and she looks great too! She has REDUCED the plastic in the bathroom. Now she uses bars of soap and shampoo instead of bottles.

Lulu and her family are RETHINKING how they shop. They buy fruit and vegetables without packaging. They take their own container to fill up with pasta and flour.

OCEAN ACTION

We can all make changes to our lives to slow down climate change. Can you think of ways you can REDUCE, REUSE AND RECYCLE. Are there things that you could RETHINK and do in a new way?

A Good Catch

We can help maintain the biodiversity of our seas by making sure the fish we eat is responsibly sourced and not from overfished stock.

Overfishing happens when fish are caught faster than they can reproduce or be replaced. Taking too many fish from our oceans disrupts food chains which will have an impact on the entire marine ecosystem.

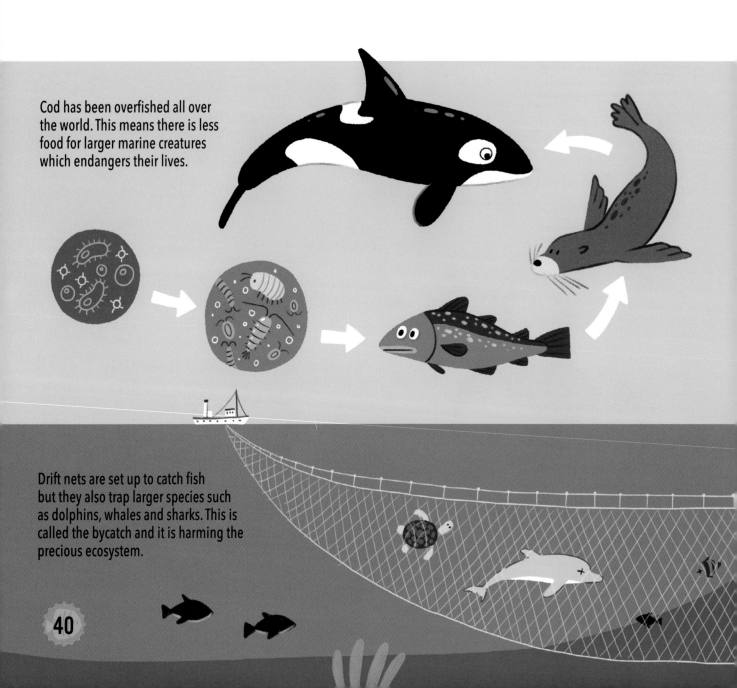

Cod has been overfished all over the world. This means there is less food for larger marine creatures which endangers their lives.

Drift nets are set up to catch fish but they also trap larger species such as dolphins, whales and sharks. This is called the bycatch and it is harming the precious ecosystem.

The school cook, Mr Lee, makes sure that the tuna he feeds the children is caught using pole and line. The pole and line method means that fishermen catch one fish at a time, avoiding harm to other marine life. It also means that fishermen throw back the younger fish.

The children are eating fish and chips for dinner. They only buy from a shop which sells responsibly-sourced cod.

The World on a Cliff Edge

Ms Barker has organised a fun school trip to the sea. High on the cliffs the children can see seabirds making nests – and lots of noise!

Their teacher explains that the cliffs are the birds' natural habitat. These steep cliffs are made from limestone. Every year part of the cliffs crumbles into the sea because of erosion. Erosion is caused by the wind and the waves as they crash against the land.

Some of the houses look really close to the edge of the cliff. Ms Barker says that some homes on cliffs are lost every year because of cliff erosion. Erosion is happening quicker because of rising sea levels.

The eroded sand, pebbles and other material is moved by the sea up and down the coast in a process called transportation. This can damage the coastal environment for people, plants and animals.

Sometimes, it feels like the whole world is on a cliff edge. We need to make changes to our lives now to help slow down global warming and stop the seas from rising ...

The children jump and play hide-and-seek in the sand dunes. Ms Barker explains that these are natural defences against erosion. The dunes are home to animals and plants so we need to protect these areas too.

SEA FACT

Common methods of preventing coastal erosion include: building seawalls, building groins, breakwaters and jetties or planting vegetation which will stop the sand from being transported by the sea. Another new way to tackle coastal erosion is to deposit more sand on beaches in vulnerable areas. This method is called sandscaping and it helps to protect natural habitats and homes.

Save the Seas Now

Now it's time for the children to have some fun.

Noah gets on his surfboard. He thinks of the power in the waves and the ways that power could be harnessed for our energy needs.

Anjali is swimming. The water feels lovely and warm. Every year it feels just that bit warmer. The summers are hotter too with longer heat waves. She thinks about how the world is changing.

Ms Barker has left her surfboard at home today. Instead, she smiles as she watches the children enjoy the ocean and all it has to offer. Like the rest of the green team, she's determined to do her bit to help save our seas.

Mason likes exploring rock pools. He uses his net to take a closer look but always puts creatures back.

OCEAN ACTION

Some of the ingredients used in sun cream can damage coral reefs or harm sea creatures. Look out for reef-safe sun cream which doesn't contain these harmful chemicals.

Lulu runs her hand through the golden sand. She imagines what the world will be like in 50 years' time. Will children be able to sit here on a sunny day and enjoy themselves like this?

OCEAN ACTION

If you visit the seaside, dispose of litter and plastic responsibly. Think carefully about which shells you are allowed to collect – in some countries it's illegal to take shells home.

Glossary

Acidification When the ocean absorbs carbon dioxide a chemical reaction occurs which makes the water more acidic and harmful to coral reefs and other living organisms

Algae A group of living organisms that contain chlorophyll. Algae are found all over the Earth but mostly in water.

Beachcomb To search the seashore for shells, pebbles and other treasures from the sea

Biodegradable A material that can be broken down or decomposed by bacteria or other living organisms in soil or water

Biodiversity The variety of living things, including plants, animals and insects, that live in any habitat

Carbon dioxide A colourless gas which is produced by all animals when they breathe out. It is produced by plants during photosynthesis and when materials that contain carbon, such as fossil fuels, are burned

Climate change The long-term changes to the Earth's weather patterns

Coastal erosion The removal of the sand or stones that make up beaches, dunes or cliffs near the sea, by the waves of the sea

Contaminated When something is polluted by another chemical - ie after an oil spill, the ocean has been contaminated by oil

Coral reef A rocky ridge in the sea formed by sea animals called corals

Drought A long period of very low rainfall which leads to a shortage of water

Ecosystem The community of living things and the non-living aspects (such as soil, rocks, water and climate) that make up a certain area or region. Everything in an ecosystem is linked through the food chain and energy cycles.

Earthquake Movements deep within the Earth cause the surface to shake and sometimes crack

Estuary The wide lower part of a river where it meets the sea

Flotsam and jetsam Floating bits of wreckage or debris from a ship or objects thrown from a ship that end up on the beach

Food chain Within each ecosystem smaller creatures often become food for a larger animal which in turn becomes food for an even bigger animal. Energy and nutrients are passed along the food chain this way.

Fossil fuels Natural fuel, such as coal, oil or gas, that was created from the remains of living things from a long time ago

Global warming The rise in temperature of the Earth that is causing climate change

Greenhouse gases Gases in the Earth's atmosphere that trap radiation from the Sun which creates 'the greenhouse effect' and global warming

Gravity The invisible force that pulls objects towards each other. The gravity of the moon pulls the water of the oceans.

Hurricane A large rotating tropical storm that forms over the Atlantic ocean. It has strong destructive winds

Lobster pot A trap for catching lobsters

Mangrove forest A coastal ecosystem where tropical trees with a dense root system grow

Microbeads Solid plastic particles measuring less than 1 mm in diameter that are often used in cosmetics and cleaning products. These are washed away down the sink from our homes via the sewers into our waterways and oceans.

Microfibres The fine fibres that are shed from manmade fabrics such as polyester

Microplastics Small plastic pieces or particles from broken down pieces of household or industrial plastic

Phytoplankton Microscopic plants living in our seas

Plankton Microscopic living organisms, both plants and animals, living in freshwater or the sea

Renewable Something that can be replaced naturally - renewable energy includes solar, wind and hydro

Reservoir A large natural or man-made lake which acts as a water supply

Tsunami A series of large waves that hit the land caused by earthquakes at sea.

Typhoon A large, destructive tropical storm that forms over the Indian or western Pacific oceans.

 # Find out more

Friends of the Earth
https://friendsoftheearth.uk

An international organisation which champions green causes and helps to protect our natural world including our oceans. You can join local campaigns to reduce plastic use in your area as well as protect nature and the seas.

Greenpeace
www.greenpeace.org.uk

Join the worldwide charity which actively fights to save our seas. Its numerous campaigns include fighting climate change, defending the oceans from plastic pollution, campaigning for sustainable fishing and promoting ocean sanctuaries.

Sea Shepherd UK
www.seashepherd.org.uk/

This charity sends volunteer divers to collect discarded fishing nets - the deadly 'ghost nets' which are so harmful to marine life. Sea Shepherd also campaigns against the culling of sea creatures all around the world.

Surfers against Sewage
www.sas.org.uk/

Join a team of surfers and volunteers who campaign for cleaner oceans and do their bit by organising beach cleans and fun fundraising events.

WWF
www.wwf.org.uk

WWF fight against plastic pollution, acidification, overfishing, coastal development and more. You can do your bit to help by becoming a member and adding your voice to petitions to governments everywhere.

Index